S0-BJN-621

Power and Persuasion in Media and ADVERTISING

Susan Brophy Down

CRABTREE
PUBLISHING COMPANY
WWW.CRABTREEBOOKS.COM

Author: Susan Brophy Down

Editors: Ellen Rodger and Janine Deschenes

Proofreader: Roseann Biederman

Design, photo research, and prepress: Katherine Berti

Cover design: Ken Wright

Print coordinator: Katherine Berti

Photo credits:
Alamy
Best View Stock: p. 25 (top)
dpa picture alliance: p. 41 (top)
Richard Levine: p. 37
The Advertising Archives: p. 36 (left)
urbanbuzz: p. 11
ZUMA Press, Inc.: p. 24
Shutterstock
1000 Words: p. 9
alredosaz: p. 13
Andreas Marquardt: p. 31
ArthurStock: p. 6 (phone)
Asia Travel: p. 34 (top)
chrisdorney: p. 30 (chocolate)
Delpixel: p. 41 (bottom)
Denys Prykhodov: p. 6 (tablet)
Ekaterina_Minaeva: p 40 (bottom)
emka74: p. 35 (left)
f11photo: p. 1
Gritsana P: p. 42
Hi-Point: p. 20 (center left)
Keith Homan: p. 40 (center)
Kondoruk: p. 6 (newspapers)
Luciano Mortula: p. 28
Nagel Photography: p. 20 (top left)
Roman Tiraspolsky: p. 36 (right)
s_bukley: p. 35 (right)
Sarunyu L: p. 34 (bottom)
Sheila Fitzgerald: p. 30 (cereal bar)
Sorbis: p. 30 (center right)
spatuletail: p. 20 (bottom)
Thinglass: p. 23 (bottom left)
Toronto-Images.com: p. 4
Yulia Reznikov: p. 6 (magazine)
All other images by Shutterstock

Library and Archives Canada Cataloguing in Publication

Down, Susan Brophy, author
Power and persuasion in media and advertising / Susan Brophy Down.

(Why does media literacy matter?)
Includes bibliographical references and index.
Issued in print and electronic formats.
ISBN 978-0-7787-4544-0 (hardcover).--
ISBN 978-0-7787-4548-8 (softcover).--
ISBN 978-1-4271-2040-3 (HTML)

1. Advertising--Psychological aspects--Juvenile literature. 2. Advertising and children--Juvenile literature. 3. Advertising--Juvenile literature. 4. Persuasion (Psychology)--Juvenile literature. 5. Mass media--Influence--Juvenile literature. 6. Mass media--Psychological aspects--Juvenile literature. I. Title.

HF5829.D69 2018 j659.101'9 C2017-908100-4
C2017-908101-2

Library of Congress Cataloging-in-Publication Data

Names: Down, Susan Brophy, author.
Title: Power and persuasion in media and advertising / Susan Brophy Down.
Description: New York : Crabtree Publishing Company, [2018]
Series: Why does media literacy matter?
Includes bibliographical references and index.
Identifiers: LCCN 2017060377 (print)
LCCN 2018002644 (ebook)
ISBN 9781427120403 (Electronic)
ISBN 9780778745440 (hardcover)
ISBN 9780778745488 (pbk.)
Subjects: LCSH: Advertising--Psychological aspects--Juvenile literature. | Mass media--Psychological aspect--Juvenile literature. | Media literacy--Juvenile literature.
Classification: LCC HF5822 (ebook) | LCC HF5822 .D69 2018 (print) | DDC 659.1/042--dc23
LC record available at https://lccn.loc.gov/2017060377

Crabtree Publishing Company

www.crabtreebooks.com 1-800-387-7650

Printed in the U.S.A./052018/BG20180327

Published in Canada
Crabtree Publishing
616 Welland Ave.
St. Catharines, Ontario
L2M 5V6

Published in the United States
Crabtree Publishing
PMB 59051
350 Fifth Avenue, 59th Floor
New York, New York 10118

Published in the United Kingdom
Crabtree Publishing
Maritime House
Basin Road North, Hove
BN41 1WR

Published in Australia
Crabtree Publishing
3 Charles Street
Coburg North
VIC, 3058

Table of Contents

Ads All Around Us

Look around you. Do you see any advertisements? Think back on your day so far. What ads have you seen? Were there clothing or beauty commercials on your TV this morning? Did an ad for a new phone app play before you watched a YouTube video of your favorite blogger? Did the blogger speak about any products in the video? What about those flyers on your doorstep or the billboard you saw on your way to school?

Everywhere We Look

Advertisements, or ads, are any kind of public announcement—from written statements to images and videos—that aim to sell a certain **product** or **service**. Advertisements are paid for by the company or person that is selling the product or service. There are advertising messages everywhere we look.

You're probably used to seeing advertising for all kinds of products on familiar channels such as TV, newspapers, and online. But when you look for it, you can see advertisements on places such as park benches, grocery carts, or your favorite YouTube channel. Some advertising comes in disguise. Enter a contest, complete a survey, or play a game online and you are probably being persuaded to buy a product.

Advertising Power

It makes sense that advertisements are such a big part of our lives. As **consumers**, we buy products and services from around the world every day. Advertisements are the way that companies can tell us about their products and services. But advertisements can also have a negative effect. People who design ads want to convince others to buy their product or service—sometimes at any cost. Some ads reflect **stereotypes**, send harmful messages, or **embellish** the truth to make people want to purchase a product.

Powerful and **persuasive**, advertising is a strong force in our lives, whether we realize it or not. That's why it is so critical to learn about the strategy and creativity behind the ads. If you have ever tried to sell something using an online ad, then you know the importance of making every word and image as compelling as possible. What words do you use to attract a buyer? Maybe you describe your old, worn desk as being "solid wood," or "in excellent condition." You might take a photo and then adjust it using computer programs (or an Instagram filter) so people can't see the scratches. You might sell your desk using these strategies, but have you been honest?

Selling Happiness

A company that sells teeth-whitening toothpaste might run an ad that shows a group of friends smiling confidently. The ad would feature pearly-white smiles. But what is it really saying?

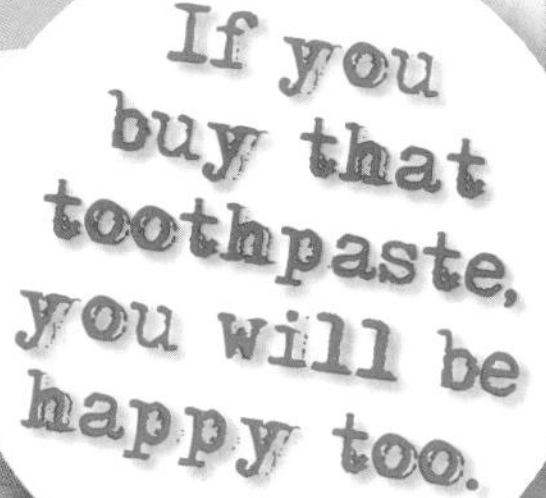

Information Channels Open

We get information through many **media channels**, or types. Media is the plural of the word **medium**, which is a way that information is spread around the world. Some of the main media channels are:

- News media, such as newspapers, magazines, TV news stations, radio, and online news websites
- Print media, such as books, novels, newspapers, magazines, and comics
- Entertainment media, such as movies, TV shows, videos, and computer games
- Online media, such as blogs, podcasts, and websites such as YouTube
- Social media, such as Facebook, Instagram, SnapChat, and Twitter

One person, group, or company can reach many others through different media channels. Companies print millions of newspaper and magazine copies. Information is **broadcasted** to millions of people through the radio or television. Online articles can be posted, shared, and sent all over the world in an instant. This type of "one-to-many" communication is called **mass communication**.

Advertising uses mass communication to get their product or service seen by many people. Ads take up space in the media channels you see—from the commercial breaks during your favorite TV show to the ads you are forced to watch before YouTube videos begin.

Ads usually have a **slogan**, an image, and an argument about why the product is good. But advertising is changing because of changes in technology, and how we get our information. Have you ever seen a celebrity or popular person on your social media feed promoting a product? How many followers do they have who may see their promotion? The Internet allows advertisers to reach many people all at once, just like traditional media channels.

> "Don't sell the steak, sell the sizzle!"
>
> Elmer Wheeler, marketing expert, 1937

What is Media and Information Literacy?

Basic literacy means you can read and write well enough to interpret signs, fill out forms, and follow written instructions—all skills necessary in everyday life.

If you are literate, you can read the clever slogans in advertising such as "Just Do It" for Nike. But you need another set of literacy skills to analyze and understand the many media messages coming at you constantly.

Media literacy means you understand how the media works, you can identify and explain different types of media, analyze how different types of media create meaning, and evaluate the effect that media has on yourself and others. Being media literate also means that you can create media content of your own.

Information literacy is the ability to find information you need, organize it, and use it in the right way. For example, if you are thinking about buying a product, you might research more information about it and use that information to make your decision.

Why does Media Literacy Matter?

Media literacy can help you make sense of all of the advertisements thrown at you each day. It can help you understand how the advertising industry works to send you messages that convince you to buy products and services. It can give you the tools to think critically about the messages in the advertisements you see in the media, watch out for false claims and bad information, and evaluate products and services fairly.

Think twice—do you really need those jeans? Being media literate means that you can identify the strategies advertisers use to convince you to buy their product or service.

CHAPTER 1

You, the Consumer

SALE!

NEW IMPROVED

Every day, people see hundreds of advertising messages, from logos on a friend's T-shirt to huge billboards. Advertising comes at us through channels such as TV, print, and mobile apps.

Ads are like darts and you are the bull's-eye. That's because you are a **consumer**. You use, or consume, products such as the breakfast you eat in the morning, the pens you bring to school, and the videos you watch. Consumers are people who buy products and services for their own personal use.

For a business to be successful, it must sell its products, such as soap or cars, or services, such as bike repairs, Internet connections, or airline flights, to consumers like you. Each product or service has a **target audience**. This is the main group of people that the company wants to sell the product or service to. Check out Chapter 3 to learn more about how ads target consumers like you.

How do companies sell their products and services? First, they have to get your attention. This is where advertisements come in. Companies have a **marketing** plan for communicating with you and other consumers. Marketing activities can include **public relations**, which involves telling stories about the company's **brand** or dealing with the company's image in the public eye; and advertising, which is a way to tell you about a product or service and then give you reasons why you should buy it. Companies that produce similar products or offer similar services, such as those that make smartphones or offer a food-delivery service, are in competition with one another for consumers, like you. Just like running a race, they are in a contest to see who can win more customers.

Which items stand out to you as you walk down the aisle of a supermarket? Food companies are in competition with one another to make you pick their item off the shelf.

Rhetoric: Logos, Ethos, and Pathos

Because companies are trying so hard to convince you to buy their product or service, advertising messages are highly creative. They might show flashy images, use catchy songs, or feature celebrities and sports stars—all to grab your attention and influence you to become a customer. These creative ads want to make you think positively about their company and the product or service they are selling.

But ads also have more subtle means of influencing the way you think about their product or service. They use language called **rhetoric** to make consumers think or feel a certain way. Rhetoric is persuasive language, meant to influence the way others think or act. Rhetoric is often split into three categories, organized by which type of evidence is used to convince the audience of something. These categories are logos, to argue using logic or facts; ethos, to argue using ethics and trust; and pathos, to argue using emotions.

Logos

This is a logical argument full of facts that convince you to buy a product. Advertising that uses logos might state that the product came first in a competition or on a survey. Maybe it is a paper towel that is more absorbent, or a phone plan that has more data. An ad might use numbers, such as "90 percent of dentists recommend this toothpaste." This approach commonly uses comparison words such as "better" or "improved."

Ads that use pathos want to make consumers feel a certain way. The emotion an ad shows depends on the target audience. Ads targeted at young children often try to make them feel happy or excited, so that parents will be convinced that the product will make their child happy.

Ethos

This is an argument that appeals to your sense of trust by using a testimonial, which is a personal opinion about a product. These ads convince people that a product is good by using reliable people to tell them about it. For example, you would trust a doctor who described how effective a type of cough medicine is. Some ads even use real people because consumers have been shown to trust people who are similar to them.

Pathos

These ads persuade us by making us feel a certain way. They appeal to our emotions such as fear and love. An ad might show a child giving a box of chocolates to her grandmother—sending the message that the chocolate is a sign of love. Another ad might urge you to donate to a pet shelter by showing photos of neglected animals. This kind of ad hopes to use your sympathy for the animals to gather support for the shelter.

Advertising often uses all three approaches to reach consumers. Let's say you want to see a movie. How do you choose one? An ad might use logos by informing you that the movie won five Golden Globe awards. The ad might also have positive reviews from movie critics or from regular people, which is an example of ethos. Finally, the ad might show you short clips from the movie. These are usually action-packed or emotional scenes, showing a character who is facing challenges. This is an appeal to your emotions, as you want to find out what happens to that character.

Can you identify how this movie poster uses rhetoric?

An ad for a candy or drink might use a cartoon superhero or silly actor for a commercial that has nothing to do with the taste of the product. Can you think of an example? What kind of rhetoric does this type of ad use? Why do you think companies choose to advertise their products in this way?

The overt message in this ad is that the laundry detergent will make your clothing clean again.

Meeting Our Needs

People need to meet their basic needs for air, water, food, and shelter. Once they are met, we are motivated to **fulfill** other needs, such as belonging and love. We want to belong to a social group, feel accepted by our families, and feel proud of ourselves. Advertisers know how to use these motivations to convince us that buying certain products or services will meet these needs.

This advertisement for sunglasses shows cool, relaxed teens wearing unique sunglass styles. It implies that people who wear the sunglasses have a fun, carefree lifestyle.

Overt and Implied Messages

There are two main types of messages found in advertising. **Overt** messages are clear and easy to understand. In an ad, they are the main message that tells you to buy a product or service. A grocery store ad might show photos of food next to their prices. This is an overt message that states the item for sale and its cost.

Implied messages are hints or suggestions that are not directly stated. That same grocery store ad could have an image showing a family eating fruits and vegetables at a picnic. The implied message in this image is that shopping at the store will help families eat healthy and have fun.

Many ads use implied messages to sell a certain **lifestyle** to consumers. A lifestyle is a way of living—such as healthy, active, professional, or carefree lifestyles. Advertisers know that people want to have a lifestyle that makes them happy, fulfills their needs, and is accepted by others. So they create ads that show certain lifestyles to try to appeal to the people who follow—or want to follow—that lifestyle. The ads imply that if consumers buy the product or service, they are part of that lifestyle too.

Can You Get the Message?

The Wonderful Company sells healthy food products such as fruit, nuts, flowers, and juices. One of their products is called Wonderful Pistachios. The company advertises pistachios as a healthy snacking option for people who are health-conscious. According to the company's vice president of marketing in 2017, Wonderful Pistachios is the fastest-growing salty snack.

The Wonderful Company recently bought billboard space in Times Square, which is pictured below. The ad reads "The Mindful Nut." Look at the pictures, words, colors, and design of the ad. Write down the overt message the ad is sending. Then brainstorm some ideas about the ad's implied messages. What hints or suggestions can you identify? How is this advertisement selling a lifestyle? Why do you think the company has had such large success with its pistachio sales?

Visual Codes

Ever seen that red street sign with eight sides? Even without the word STOP on it, you would recognize it as a familiar symbol. And you would understand the meaning: when you are driving a car or riding a bike, you must stop at the sign. Advertisements have special symbols and codes as part of their messages, too. Here are some of them:

Logos	Logos are symbols that represent the whole company. They can be words or letters in a certain color or creative shape, or they can be **icons** or graphic designs. Apple Computers, McDonald's, and Shell Oil are companies with easily recognizable logos. In advertisements, logos help you identify the company—and also recognize it in your daily life, making you a possible buyer.
Colors	Colors are important symbols in ads. Green is associated with nature, so a detergent that is safe for the environment might use green in its ad. A serious ad for a bank or insurance company might have blues and grays, but a product that is fun, such as a candy or a toy, would use attention grabbing red or yellow. Products inspired by a different country, such as Italian pasta sauce or Mexican taco shells, might use the colors from that country's flag in the ads.
Photography	Camera angles are important parts of an ad. Most models in cosmetic ads gaze directly into your eyes. This is meant to send the message that the model is being honest. In other ads, the camera angle may be from your point of view—such as those inside a car, or looking down at a product.
Body language	Wink. Shrug your shoulders. Smile. Those are all body language messages. The models in ads use body language to show happiness or confidence. Body language in ads also shows fear or sadness—emotions that are usually fixed by the product or service being sold. The expressions are often exaggerated to show you how the product can improve your life.

These are just some of the strategies that advertisers use to reach you with their messages. Next you will find out how advertising started and where it is going!

Pavlov's Dogs

Do you get hungry when you hear an advertising jingle for a restaurant? That's the goal of advertisers, who hope that your brain will automatically make the connection between a product and its visual or auditory ad. This idea is based on research by a Russian biologist named Ivan Pavlov. He noticed that his dogs started drooling when their handler entered the kennel, because they knew he was going to feed them. Pavlov wondered if he could change the dogs' behavior and make them respond to a completely different sight or sound that was not related to feeding at all. In his experiment, Pavlov rang a bell before the dogs' feeding time. Pretty soon, the dogs learned that the noise meant food was coming. They began to drool when they heard the bell. Pavlov called this reaction **classical conditioning**. Can you think of conditioned responses you have to certain smells or sounds?

What conditioned responses do you have to these images of food advertisements?

Think of two competing companies or brands. Perhaps it is two running shoe brands or two department stores. Look at their ads and websites. What messages are they sending to consumers? How are they different in their approach?

Creating Advertising

Anger. Shyness. Excitedness. Those are some of the actions and emotions that make up human behavior. Several things—including your attitudes and beliefs, your personality, and your culture—influence how you behave.

The environment in which you live also affects your behavior. Humans are social creatures, which means that other people and your need to fit in with them influence the way you behave. Media can also affect human behavior. Media psychology is the study of how media, from video games to ads and movies, can influence how you understand and react to situations.

Advertising media can influence our perception of ourselves and each other. For example, advertising stereotypes that show women acting or looking a certain way can influence how we think about gender roles. An ad showing women cleaning up after the whole family, or a man struggling to do simple housework, supports the stereotypical idea that women excel at housework and family care, while men do not. Ads that show thin female models or muscular male models can make viewers believe that these are how men and women should look.

Some media psychology theories say that the media affects our thoughts because our brains sometimes process media images as real memories.

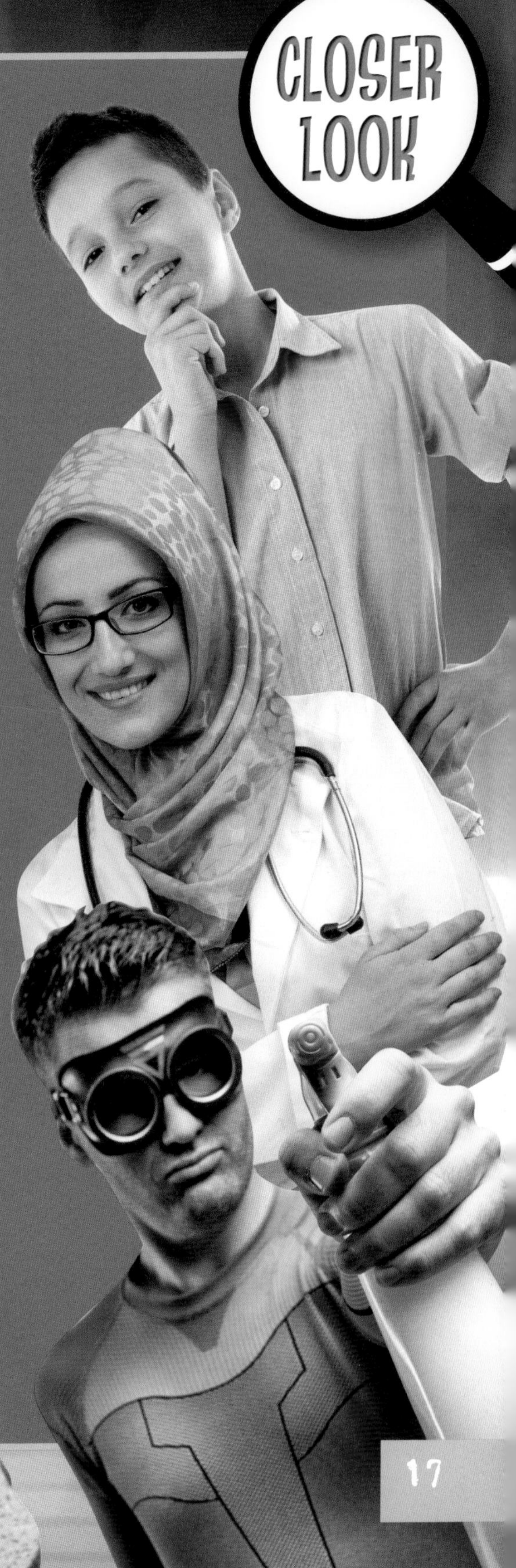

The Unstereotype Alliance

Some of the world's biggest organizations and brands have recognized how advertising media can contribute to stereotypes about males and females—and, in 2017, banded together to stop it. The new effort is called the Unstereotype Alliance, which aims to remove gender-based stereotypes in ads around the world. It was created in part by UN Women, the part of the **United Nations** (UN) that works for the empowerment of females, the large health and hygiene company Unilever, and other huge companies such as Facebook, Google, and Proctor & Gamble.

Part of the motivation to create the alliance came from research done by Unilever in 2016. The researchers found that 40 percent of women did not feel the women they saw in ads represented them. The researchers also found that just 3 percent of advertisements featured women in managerial or professional roles. Instead, women were often shown in secondary and service roles, and were also presented in ways that emphasized their bodies or beauty.

The Unstereotype Alliance has already influenced a change in many ads. Unilever changed a Knorr food ad showing a woman and daughter in the kitchen to a man and his son. Unilever-owned Axe body spray changed the implied messages in its commercials from "Axe can help boys get a girlfriend" to "Axe can help all people be confident in their individuality." Another notable example is Audi's 2017 Super Bowl commercial. It promotes equal pay for men and women and features a young girl winning a soapbox derby.

The UN believes that by changing the ways men and women are presented in ads, advertisers can play a large role in changing stereotypes around the world.

The Marketing Industry

Advertising companies work hard to make sure you recognize, or remember, their brands. How many of the brands below do you recognize?

Ads are everywhere, so it must be a huge business, right? Right! The advertising industry was estimated at $600 billion USD in revenue in 2015. TV is still important, but more ads are shifting to online and mobile, and away from older channels such as newspapers.

In the last 20 years, the industry has **consolidated**. This means that larger companies have swallowed up many small advertising **agencies**. The biggest companies have offices all over the world. Among the largest are: Omnicom Group and Interpublic Group (based in New York City), WPP Group (based in London, UK), Publicis Groupe (based in Paris, France), and Dentsu (based in Japan). These global companies make billions of dollars every year—off of convincing customers like you to buy products and services.

Message to Action

Advertisers know that convincing you to become a customer is a long process. Even the most creative ads don't work right away. Usually, there are five steps toward becoming a customer of a company. The steps begin with an advertisement.

Step 1 Awareness	It may take many ads or a campaign on social media before you notice the product. Some studies say people must see an ad seven times before they pay attention to the message.
Step 2 Interest	Once you hear about the product, you might want to know more. So you might go to the website to look for other information.
Step 3 Analysis	You figure out whether the product is right for you, sometimes by asking friends. Is it a reasonable price? Is it the right size or color?
Step 4 Trial	You may use a sample handed out at the store, try out a friend's product, or see a demonstration of a new gadget.
Step 5 Regular Use	You finally decide to buy the product, and if you become a fan, you may be the one telling others about it all.

Think about the last product or service you chose to buy. How did you hear about it? What steps led you to decide to buy it?

Evolution of Ads

Thousands of years ago, the first advertisements were posted in a public place for everyone to see. Sometimes ad messages were written right on the walls like graffiti.

After the **printing press** was invented, advertising grew. In the 18th century, many new factories and stores offered goods you could buy rather than make yourself. As it became possible for factories to make products in huge quantities in the 19th and 20th centuries, companies reached out beyond the local village markets to find larger numbers of consumers. To let many people know about these widely-available products, companies began to advertise. But because there were so many magazines and newspapers, especially in cities, new companies called advertising agencies were created to give advice to the companies. The ad agencies created ad ideas for the companies.

The ad agencies hire writers and artists to create the eye-catching ads and write the messages that make us want to buy. They also decide where to place the ads so that a large number of target consumers will see it. Where an ad is placed depends on the type of product and the target audience. For example, if the product is a woman's dress, the agency might place the ad in a women's magazine or on a website popular with women.

"Over time, advertising has gained the reputation of pollution content. We have to now create content that consumers want."

Brad Jakeman,
beverage executive

Advertising Through the Years

Advertising is all around us today, but its evolution from simple wall messages and posted notices took thousands of years. Here are some highlights since Gutenberg's printing press:

1440s	Johannes Gutenberg invents new movable type printing press
1700s	Josiah Wedgwood pioneers **direct marketing** in UK for his pottery business
1742	Benjamin Franklin prints magazine ads in US
1830s	First newspaper advertising appears in France. The publisher realizes he can sell papers more cheaply because of the advertising money he earns. Other papers quickly copy the idea.
1830s	First billboards appear as circus posters in New York City
1840s	First advertising agencies are formed
1872	Department store Montgomery Ward creates first mail-order catalog
1880s	Pears Soap pioneers advertising in UK. Ivory Soap is advertised for first time in US.
1892	Sears sends first mail ad campaign directly to customers
1899	American ad agency J. Walter Thompson becomes the first to go international with London office
1900s	New US laws against advertising fake medicine that promised miracle cures
1920s	Commercial radio, or radio broadcasts owned by private companies, begins
1930s	Public service announcements, or free government ads, appear
1935	American Institute for Public Opinion founded as first market researcher
1941	First TV ad in US
1971	Ban on cigarette advertising on TV and radio in US
1988	Nike's ad agency creates "Just Do It" slogan
2000s	Canada and US set up Do Not Call lists to restrict telemarketers
2004	Dove Campaign for Real Beauty begins
2007	Social media ads appear

The Channels

Advertisers choose different media channels to reach consumers. Here are some of the channels they use, and reasons why each one is effective.

Direct response	These ads include coupons and flyers, often called junk mail, telemarketing, and e-mail marketing. These reach people directly and cheaply.
Internet	Internet ads can include those on your social media, pop-ups before videos, and sidebars on websites and blogs. These are inexpensive ads, and often companies can use information from the websites to track how the ad is performing—or how many people are clicking on it.
Out-of-home (OOH)	Billboards, bus shelters, arenas, and airplane banners are examples of this type of ad. These are effective in big cities or where large groups gather, as many people can see them at once.
Broadcast	These ads include TV and radio. These are expensive ads to produce, but they do a good job of showing and appealing to emotions.
Mobile	These are ads on websites or games, such as Oreo's popular game app in which players dunk the cookie into milk. These ads familiarize people with the company name.
Print	These are regular ads in newspapers and magazines as well as native ads. Native ads are content that look like they are part of a story, but an advertiser pays for them. For example, a story about travel destinations might recommend certain restaurants to visit or activities to try in certain places—but the companies that own them paid for these recommendations. Consumers say print ads are the most logical and believable.

As technology and people's habits change, marketers are looking for new ways to advertise. Ad blocking software and PVRs, which allow people to record TV shows and fast-forward through ads, make it easier to ignore or eliminate ads. That's why advertisers are always creating different types of advertising.

Magic Words of Advertising

There are a few magic words that most advertising messages use to persuade you:

Free	As well as meaning no cost, free can also be used as a compound word (germ-free, calorie-free). What lifestyles do these compound words imply?
Save	If it isn't free, then save is the next best thing.
Easy	It should be easy to learn, use, or put together.
Now	Why wait?
New	In other words, get rid of the old one.
Proven	You can trust it.
Results	It sounds scientific.
Best	In other words, you made the right choice.
Love	You won't just like this product...
You	That is the most important word, because you are who the ad wants to reach!

Keep a log of all the ads you see in one day. Create a chart to organize the ads by each channel you see them in. Which channel do you see the most ads in? Which channel do you see the least? Why do you think that is? Do you think the channels in which you see ads will change as you get older?

Direct response	||
Internet	𝍸 |
Out-of-home	|||
Broadcast	𝍸 ||||
Mobile	𝍸
Print	||

Guerrilla Marketing

Advertising is all about grabbing attention. Sometimes companies use a special kind of public relations called **guerrilla marketing** to grab consumers' attention in unique, memorable ways. Guerilla marketing is very different from the conventional ads you see on media channels. Instead, companies aim for big attention (for free) by creating a stunt or a prank. These events are so unusual that the media reports them as news and the videos may go viral on social media. Stunts can sometimes have much more impact than buying ad space, as it makes the company memorable—and the news coverage can reach a wider range of people.

One example is Canadian airline WestJet, whose 2013 stunt earned more than 36 million views on YouTube in its first year. The airline employees asked passengers what they wanted for Christmas before they boarded their flight, and then had the items delivered on the luggage carousel at their destination.

Coca-Cola installed a specially-designed vending machine at St. John's University in New York in 2010. When students put coins in the machine, it dispensed much more Coke than was expected as well as pizza, flowers, and a huge submarine sandwich to share. This was part of the Happiness Machine campaign, and the video went viral on social media.

When California's Universal Studios wanted to advertise its new King Kong 3D attraction in 2010, they dug giant ape footprints in the sand at nearby Santa Monica beach, and placed a crushed lifeguard's vehicle beside them, suggesting that the fictional movie ape was on a frightening rampage. The stunt drew attention to the new ride.

Consumers are more likely to buy a product when they remember it! Advertisers work very hard to make their ads memorable, using creative methods such as guerrilla marketing. The successful iPod advertisements featuring dancing silhouettes are considered to be some of the most visually memorable of the 2000s.

> Nobody counts the number of ads you run; they just remember the impression you make.
>
> Bill Bernbach, advertising executive

DIG DEEP

You want to advertise a new brand of shoes that you hope will be popular with youth 10-18 years old. Through which media channels will you reach your audience? What magic words and interesting images will you use to send your message? What kind of lifestyle will you sell? How will you make your ad memorable? Use the strategies you have learned in this book so far to create your ad.

Targeting You

Mass marketing used to be the only way to advertise. That meant that advertisers created one message for everybody and used mainstream media channels like TV to get the messages to us. That still works for some products that we all buy. But not all consumers can be lumped into one group. Different products and services are made and provided for different groups.

How do Advertisers Identify You?

Seniors and teenagers both like ice cream, but they probably want different flavors when they go to buy some, and will be interested in and persuaded by different types of ads. That means an ice cream company needs to create different ad messages to target different consumer groups. That's why when companies create a product, they must identify their target audiences or **target markets**: the groups most likely to buy their products. To do that, they research demographics, or information about population groups. Demographic information includes the age, **race**, **gender**, job, education, and location of people. Advertisers might also research information about people's life choices, such as the trips they go on, their hobbies, and their attitudes and beliefs, such as religion.

Examples of target markets could be working mothers, homeowners, college students, or children in middle-class families. For example, if the product is infant diapers, the companies will advertise to women about to be mothers or who have children.

Who makes the buying decisions in your family? Often it's you! Studies have shown that your opinion influences your family's purchases—from the foods you snack on during a family movie to the car you pile into each day. Kids often get to choose family entertainment or restaurants as well. All of this means that kids can be a big and important target for advertisers.

If advertisers are selling retirement homes, their target audience is seniors. Their ads will probably run during daytime television, when seniors are likely to be watching TV.

How do Advertisers Find You?

Now that the target markets are picked, what next? Advertisers research what media channels to use to reach them. If the target is teenagers, then the advertisers must look for magazines, TV shows, websites, or blogs that teenagers see. There are statistics on who is reading or watching that ad channel. For example, broadcasters can track how many viewers watch each program. Another source of research is census data that will show what kind of neighborhoods we live in, and groups people by such things as their income level and their education. They can use this kind of information to decide where to advertise their products.

In a higher-income neighborhood, or an area visited by a lot of money-spending tourists, you might see billboards or other ads that show expensive items.

Data Mining

Now that advertisers can track our moves online, they can pinpoint us through data mining. This is a method of sorting through **data** to look for patterns. Advertisers can learn about us by looking at data about every web search we make, and every time we use social media. One way to track online behavior is through **cookies**. These are text files sent to your computer that can track your preferences. Ever wonder why you see ads for bikes right after you have done an online search for a bike? That's why.

DIG DEEP

Whether you know it or not, you are part of a target market for something. Describe your target market and then look for ads outside that zone. Maybe it is a magazine or a TV show for older people or a show for very young children. Write down the types of ads you see and what kinds of symbols you find. If you aren't in the target market, do the ads have any effect on you?

The Power of Branding

A brand is not just one product, but a representation of the company behind it. Brand loyalty means that consumers keep supporting that company and don't look for better deals elsewhere. Branding is one way that companies target their consumers. A clothing company that targets **millennial** consumers might create a cool and unique brand based on supporting personal style and individuality. A company that creates snack foods for families might create a brand that boasts all-natural ingredients, because adult consumers often want to choose the healthiest options to feed themselves and their children. But to make a brand successful, a company has to make potential customers familiar with it.

> Your brand is what other people say about you when you are not in the room.
> Jeff Bezos, Amazon

What brands are you loyal to? Do you see any of them pictured here?

Brand Loyalty Strategies

Advertisers use some different strategies to get consumers to spend time with the brands:

Influencers	Advertisers might pay a popular blogger or a celebrity with a huge following to talk about the product. What sounds like an opinion can sometimes be an ad.
Viral ads	A Wrigley's Extra gum ad, called The Story of Sarah and Juan, showed the man sketching scenes from their romance on gum wrappers. It got millions of views, and the company invited consumers to participate by entering their own photos to be made into sketches.
Games	Cookie brand Oreo has a popular game app. They hope that spending time with the game will mean you buy that brand at the store.
Cross promotion	A new movie can be promoted with toys, fast food, or clothing. Both companies get the benefit of the ads.
Embedded ads	Also known as product placement, this is a way of including the ad right in the show's content. For example, as a major sponsor of TV show American Idol for 13 years, Coca-Cola had cups of soda with the company logo on them placed before the judges.

The *Minions* movie gained valuable advertising power by being featured on the clothing and other products in this store. In turn, the products featuring the minion images have higher sales because of the movie's popularity.

Persuasion Alert!

Watch out for these persuasion strategies in most advertising messages.

Criticizing	Criticizing competition is a familiar tactic. Ads want to convince you that their product is better than others. The product might be called "different" or "unique" which makes it sound better, even though many competing products have almost identical ingredients or are constructed in similar ways.
Testimonial	Some ads have testimonials, or personal recommendations. They could be from a person you respect such as an athlete, an actor, or a professional such as a doctor.
Bandwagon	The bandwagon approach makes you feel that everyone else has the product except you. It pressures you to join the crowd.
Senses	These messages appeal to our five senses: touch, taste, smell, hearing, and sight. Words are powerful, but advertisers know that pictures are even better. The Got Milk? campaign used aroma strips that smelled like chocolate chip cookies for ads on bus shelters.
Repetition	Do you get tired of seeing the same ad over and over? People need to see or hear an ad several times before they really pay attention. Then they might think of that product first when it is time to buy. Some fast-food companies already have millions of customers, but their ads still remind you to go there for lunch.
Weasel words	Weasel words make you believe the ad is making promises. But inserting special words allows them to wiggle out of promising miracles. These words include "may" or "up to." Think of personal care products for things such as acne or dandruff. An ad might say "Helps stop dandruff," or "Fights bad breath." Does it promise to cure these conditions? No, it "helps" or "fights."
Humor	Humor is used to make ads memorable and allow you to see them again and again without being annoyed. Humor helps the ad content get past our logical brains and appeal to our emotions. Then we may find the ad more acceptable.

Targeted Messages

Ads have a secret language, packed with messages aimed at you. Ad creators **encode** ads with overt and implied messages, symbols, and special words that appeal to their target audience and sell a certain lifestyle to them.

Think about ads targeted at youth and teens, like you. You might see a lot of images showing groups of teens having fun together, cool slogans or hashtags, and images of smiling, attractive youth wearing hip clothing or holding the latest gadgets. These advertisers know that their target audience is at an age where social relationships and self-esteem are very important—so the ads send the message that buying their product will make teens popular and happy. The advertisers also know that hashtags and other cool slogans will appeal to teens.

Compare that to advertisements aimed at adult parents. These ads often show smiling children, touching moments between family members, and stress-free adults in organized homes. The message is that buying the product or service in the ad will help parents organize their busy lives, solve problems at home, and create a happy, loving family.

If the images above and below were used in advertisements, which groups do you think they would be targeted at? What messages do the images send? Do they sell a lifestyle?

Decoding Messages

Different people have different responses to the ads they see. We, the consumers, don't just see ads; we **decode** them so we understand their meaning. We interpret or understand the messages in ads in different ways, depending on who we are and our point of view. Different age groups, genders, ethnicities or races, and cultural groups interpret media messages in different ways.

A print ad for men's clothing might show a man riding a motorcycle in a wild landscape. In North America the motorcycle sends the implied message that the man is independent, unique, and confident. But in parts of Asia, where motorcycles and scooters are common and not high-status products, a man riding a motorcycle would not seem as appealing. Would you be likely to see an image like the one on the right, which shows people in Vietnam, in a motorcycle advertisement in North America?

A poster for a new movie might show a powerful superhero in the front. His female love interest or sidekick is likely featured in the background. A teenage boy might get the message that men are powerful, and be interested to see the movie. But how might a teenage girl interpret and respond to the ad? She might get the message that the woman is not powerful, or not an important part of the movie. This message might make her less interested to see the movie.

Whitewashing

The messages that advertisements send to their target audiences are especially harmful when they reinforce stereotypes—and even attitudes such as **racism**. Whitewashing is a phenomenon in which fair skin and European features, such as straight hair and round eyes, are featured in the media as being the most beautiful. Many beauty ads show white women. The skin tones of non-white women on ads are sometimes digitally retouched to appear lighter. Non-white women are often shown in advertisements with long, straight hair.

There are skin creams and hair products that are meant to lighten skin or keep hair straight and smooth. If the target audiences for these products are non-white women and men, the message they receive is that their natural skin tone or hair is not beautiful—and that they will become more beautiful if they use these products. Although most advertising companies insist this stereotyping and racism is not intentional, as they are advertising to white women and men too, ads need to be examined critically to think about the impact they could have on different groups.

Rihanna's skin appears lighter on this 2012 magazine cover than in the picture of her taken at the MTV Video Music Awards in the same year. Most magazines emphasize that they do not purposely retouch skin tones to make them lighter. But the lighting and design chosen for cover photos often result in models' skin appearing lighter, which many people interpret as whitewashing just the same.

DIG DEEP

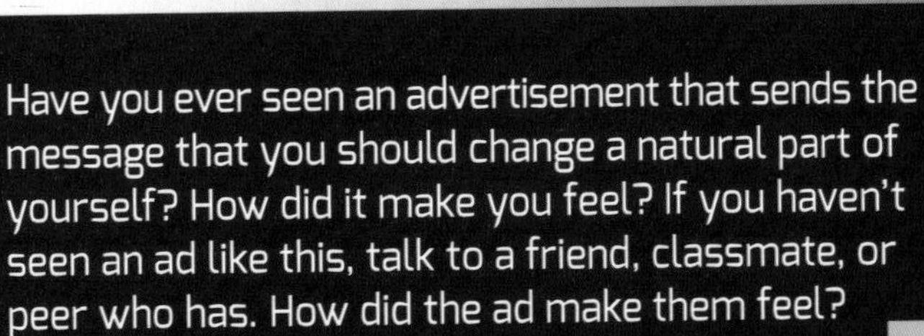

Have you ever seen an advertisement that sends the message that you should change a natural part of yourself? How did it make you feel? If you haven't seen an ad like this, talk to a friend, classmate, or peer who has. How did the ad make them feel?

Real People?

Not many women and girls think they are beautiful, according to a study that asked women in 10 countries. Many beauty ads show young, thin, conventionally beautiful, and white women. But Dove created a different kind of campaign to appeal to women and girls. Dove's Campaign for Real Beauty emphasizes the idea that everyone is beautiful. The advertising images featured women of all ages, sizes, and races, posing confidently in their underwear. Dove also created a series of videos to expose and fight against the self-doubt felt by women about their appearance. One, called "Evolution," shows how a model is retouched and remade to create a perfect image. This showed how unrealistic advertising images are.

Self-doubt about body image isn't limited to women only. Many ads also perpetuate ideas of the "perfect" male figure—usually tall, muscular, and masculine. Ads often show men who fit this image in positions of control at their jobs or in their life. They might also show these men being successful or confident when speaking with women. This teaches young boys and men that in order to be successful in their jobs, hobbies, and with women, they need to fit this kind of image.

Most ads for male cologne feature a handsome, muscular man who is shirtless or in a suit. He often has an attractive woman on his arm.

What message do you think this cologne ad sends to boys and men? Is it selling a lifestyle?

To relate to a wider audience, this Dove ad features women who do not work as models.

sleeveless-ready in just 7 days. Dove has asked real women to try out our new improved Dove Deodorant for seven days. The result: visibly softer and smoother underarms.

CLOSER LOOK

Beach Body Backlash

A 2015 ad by supplement company Protein World caused an angry reaction. Protein World's advertising campaign in England included images and billboards in London subway cars and stations. The posters showed a slim model in a yellow bikini. The tagline was "Are You Beach Body Ready?" People argued that the ad was offensive because it idealized only one type of body shape, suggesting that this body type is the only one acceptable for the beach. An online petition against the ad received thousands of signatures. In anger, subway riders ripped down the ads, spread graffiti, or made their own ads online to make fun of the original photos. The UK Advertising Standards Authority (ASA) got close to 400 complaints about the ads. The ASA ruled that the ad was not offensive. Instead it banned the ad because of health concerns due to its weight-loss claims.

What Do You Think?

- Decode this ad by indicating which persuasion strategies are being used. What overt and implied messages are in the ad?
- Why do you think the ads affected people differently in the US?
- Can you think of ads that show men's bodies in the same way? How do you think men would react?
- Does advertising need more rules, or should we let the public decide?

Protein World ran the same campaign in New York City a few weeks later. The ads got a few complaints but nothing like the outrage expressed in the UK. But since the campaign, the ASA has tightened rules on the use of gender stereotypes in ads.

Ethical Ads?

Advertising can be positive by informing you about new products. Ads can also be funny, memorable, and creative. But all too often, ads are manipulative and dishonest. Advertising can distort, or change, reality and exaggerate a product's power. Advertising professionals understand your emotions, and they know how to convince you to buy things you don't really need. New types of marketing can reach you through online games and other methods that promote brands, but don't seem like advertising. Advertising can also reinforce stereotypes and make groups of people see themselves in a negative light.

To protect consumers, many countries have regulations for advertising. They can restrict ads for harmful products, such as tobacco. The industry also has a code of **ethics**. This is a set of guidelines for good behavior. Advertisers and government regulators aren't the only ones with the power to change. Consumers can demand honest advertising from companies, and ask them to be open about their products.

In the US, a group called Truth in Advertising has a website that lists ad alerts, or warnings about deceptive or harmful ads. You can complain to them about something you think breaks the rules in print or broadcast. You can also use ad-blocking software for online ads.

What is Credible Marketing?

Credible marketing means creating ads that are believable and truthful. You can trust the company behind them. There are three things to look for in credible advertising:

Details	Instead of hearing **vague** statements about being improved, or beating the competition, consumers want to know the details. If they make a claim, do they verify it?
Transparency	People are naturally suspicious of claims that a product is the best or the biggest. They want to know that the company makes a good product and it is reliable.
Authenticity	To be authentic means to be genuine and truthful. Companies have websites and apps to share news from behind the scenes. Authenticity helps consumers feel like they have a relationship with the company. Authentic advertising has been very successful for some companies:

- Blendtec blenders created a series of YouTube videos that went viral. They threw garden rakes, marbles, and all kinds of things into their blender, to prove how powerful it was.
- Have you heard the tagline, "It tastes awful, but it works"? The medicine company Buckleys set themselves apart when they used honesty in their advertising for cough medicine. By admitting the product's weaknesses, the brand also became more memorable.

A 2015 study examining cosmetics ads showed that less than 20 percent were truthful. Does that mascara really make your eyelashes look like that, or is the model wearing false eyelashes?

Ethics

Advertising goes too far at times, and it can influence people in the wrong way. That's why there are regulations in advertising. How many rules there are depend on the channel—TV and radio ads have more restrictions than print. Online channels are struggling with fake ads and lack of privacy for consumers and may need more regulations.

On some subjects, most of the world agrees. In 2005, the World Health Organization recommended that countries around the world should ban advertising of tobacco products. There are strict rules about ads that can tempt people to do things that could be harmful such as drinking alcohol or gambling.

Targeting Children and Youth

For very young children under seven years old, it's hard to tell the difference between fantasy and reality. Studies have found that they may believe what they see on their televisions, including advertising, is real. Because of this, several countries, such as Norway and Sweden, have banned ads aimed at children under 12. The Canadian province of Quebec prohibits advertising aimed at children under age 13.

Many other countries have strong regulations about advertising to children. These ads aren't allowed to humiliate or show children being mocked by friends for not having a certain toy. Some ads aimed at adults can only be broadcast in the evening or at night, so children won't see them.

Toy packaging tries hard to catch the attention of young children. It often features fantasy characters, colorful pictures, and exciting settings to catch children's interest. But usually, the toy is much different from what its packaging suggests. A superhero toy can't really fly, for example.

Pushing unrealistic images on teens can influence their body image and self-esteem. Ads showing only certain body types, such as thin women and muscular men, can cause viewers to be unhealthy in trying to achieve these standards. Other ads feature gender and racial stereotypes.

A Brown Girl's Guide to Beauty

Aranya Johar began using "fairness creams" at the age of 9. The beauty advertisements she saw on TV showed light-skinned women, and the other women in her community in India also used skin products meant to lighten dark skin. She felt that her darker skin made her ugly, and struggled with the unrealistic beauty expectations she saw in the media.

So Aranya decided to speak out against the harmful beauty standards that imply that white skin is the most beautiful. She wrote and performed a spoken-word poem titled "A Brown Girl's Guide to Beauty." In the poem, she describes her experience and also the experiences of other members of her family, such as her cousin who adopted unhealthy eating habits to achieve the abs he saw in magazines. She reminds us, "We forget that beauty for men also comes with a cost." Aranya's poem ends with messages of empowerment to all people—that advertisements cannot tell people what beauty is, and that people should not determine their own beauty based on unrealistic standards in the media.

Aranya describes that in India, many women featured in the media have a lighter shade of skin. She argues that people need to value "all shapes and shades."

Greenwashing

Many people want to live healthy and environmentally-friendly lifestyles. That's why advertisers like to convince consumers that their products are eco-friendly or healthy. Unfortunately, some companies go too far when they advertise. When a product has a misleading environmental image, or an image that wrongly implies it is healthy and natural, it is called "greenwashing." Some ways that companies greenwash their products include:

Distraction	Ads might show images that go against how that product actually harms the environment. A car commercial shows a family driving in the forest in an SUV. The family might be trying to enjoy nature, but the gas a car uses is not environmentally friendly. A bottle of water says it's natural. But what about the plastic used in the bottles, most of which doesn't get recycled?
Vague claims	The word natural gets used in vague ads, whether it is shampoo or fast food. But often, there is not specific evidence provided in the ad to prove that the ingredients are natural, nor that they are good for the environment.

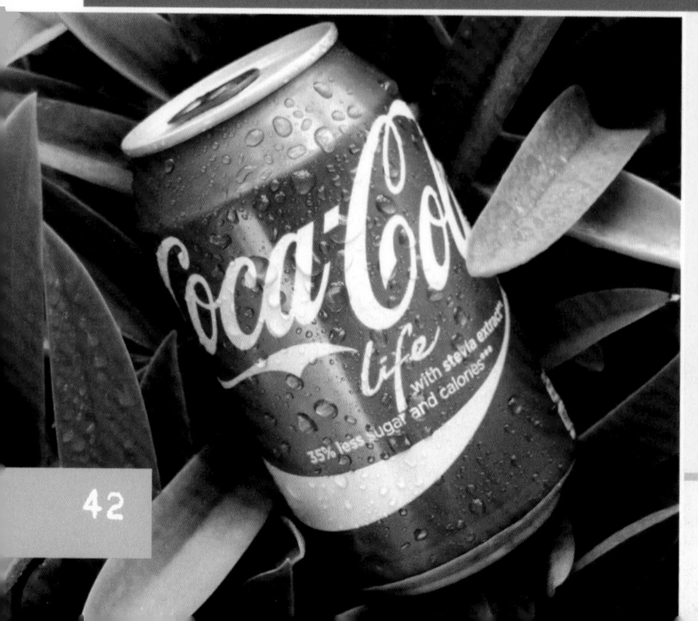

In 2014, Coca-Cola launched "Coca-Cola Life." This "new" soft drink boasted that it was sweetened using natural ingredients, and featured a green can and bottle label rather than the brand's signature red. But although the drink has fewer calories than the regular option, and does not use **artificial** sweeteners that some consider harmful, the fizzy drink is hardly natural—nor is it a healthy option for consumers. The greenwashed advertisement, however, sends the message that consumers who choose this product are drinking a natural—and therefore healthy—option.

Regulators and Advocates

In the US, the Federal Communications Commission (FCC) and the Federal Trade Commission (FTC) are regulators that watch out for scams and frauds in advertising including telemarketing and online ads.

Parts of the advertising industry in many countries are self-regulated, and advertisers agree to follow the rules voluntarily. The US has the Advertising Self-Regulatory Council, and Canada has Advertising Standards Canada. The Interactive Advertising Bureau (IAB) is a group that represents media and technology companies in more than 40 countries. It is creating standards to stop fake ads and protect people's privacy.

Once you know how to decode the messages found in advertisements, you can be a very wise consumer.

Conclusion

In this book, you have learned who makes ads, what the ads really say, and what they are persuading you to do. Remember to analyze the ads to understand explicit and implicit messages in them. When you see an ad, ask yourself:

- What is this ad selling? Is it something I need, or something I want?
- Who is this ad targeting?
- What explicit and implicit messages exist in this ad? What words, images, and symbols do they use to send those messages?
- What stereotypes exist in this ad?

Best of all, be **skeptical**, and don't forget your sense of humor. A Canadian group called Companies Committed to Kids created a **public service ad** in 1999 about The House Hippo. You can still find the "ad" on YouTube. It sounds serious, like an educational video that talks about wild animals. Except it's not true! The "House Hippo" is completely fictional. The video was meant to show that you can't believe everything you see in the media.

Bibliography

Introduction

"Media and Information Literacy." United Nations Educational, Scientific, and Cultural Organization. https://en.unesco.org/themes/media-and-information-literacy

Elmer Wheeler Web Resource. www.elmerwheeler.net

Chapter 1

Berger, Arthur Asa. "How to Analyze an Advertisement." Center for Media Literacy. www.medialit.org/reading-room/how-analyze-advertisement

Fredholm, Lotta. "Pavlov's Dog." Nobelprize.org, 2001. www.nobelprize.org/educational/medicine/pavlov/readmore.html

"Pistachio sales approaching almonds in snacking, says Wonderful exec." FreshFruitPortal.com, 2017. www.freshfruitportal.com/news/2017/07/28/pistachio-sales-approaching-almonds-snacking-says-wonderful-exec

TED Ed. "How to use rhetoric to get what you want." YouTube, 2016. www.youtube.com/watch?v=3klMM9BkW5o

"The key to media's hidden codes." TED Ed, 2012. https://ed.ted.com/lessons/the-key-to-media-s-hidden-codes

Wilcox, D., Cameron, G. & Reber, B. *Public Relations Strategies and Tactics* (11th Edition). Pearson Education Inc., Glenview IL, 2014.

Chapter 2

"5 of the Best Guerrilla Marketing Campaigns." Ambient, 2015. https://ambientww.com/guerrilla-marketing

"Ad Age Advertising Century." Ad Age, 1999. http://adage.com/article/special-report-the-advertising-century/ad-age-advertising-century-timeline/143661

"Advertisers Will Spend Nearly $600 Billion Worldwide in 2015." E-Marketer, 2014. www.emarketer.com/Article/Advertisers-Will-Spend-Nearly-600-Billion-Worldwide-2015/1011691

Doyle, Jack. "The iPod Silhouettes: 2000-2011." The Pop History Dig. 2011. http://www.pophistorydig.com/topics/ipod-silhouettes-2000-2011/

Eveleth, Rose. "How fake images change our memory and behaviour." BBC, 2012. www.bbc.com/future/story/20121213-fake-pictures-make-real-memories

"History of OOH." Outdoor Advertising Association of America, 2018. https://oaaa.org/AboutOOH/OOHBasics/HistoryofOOH.aspx

Hope, Katie. "Unilever to use 'less sexist' ads." BBC News, 2016. www.bbc.com/news/business-36595898

"Launch of Unstereotype Alliance set to eradicate outdated stereotypes in advertising." Unilever news release, 2017. www.unilever.com/news/Press-releases/2017/launch-of-unstereotype-alliance-set-to-eradicate-outdated-stereotypes-in-advertising.html

Lum, Ryan. "WestJet Airlines Creates A Christmas Miracle For Passengers." Creative Guerrilla Marketing, 2013. www.creativeguerrillamarketing.com/guerrilla-marketing/westjet-airlines-creates-christmas-miracle-passengers

Vranica, Suzanne. Advertisers Try New Tactics to Break Through to Consumers. Wall Street Journal, 2016. www.wsj.com/articles/advertisers-try-new-tactics-to-break-through-to-consumers-1466328601

Chapter 3

Allan, Robbie. "How Oreo created the #1 app in the App Store." http://carnival.io/mobile-insights/how-oreo-created-the-1-app-in-the-app-store

Dove Campaigns. www.dove.com/ca/en/stories/campaigns.html

"Evolution." www.dove.com/ca/en/stories/campaigns/evolution.html

Gianatasio, David. "Ad of the Day: Extra Gum Wraps Up One of the Year's Sweetest Love Stories." AdWeek, 2015. www.adweek.com/brand-marketing/ad-day-extra-gum-wraps-one-years-sweetest-love-stories-167437

Goodfellow, Jessica. "Dove admits it 'missed the mark' with whitewashing ad." The Drum, 2017. www.thedrum.com/news/2017/10/08/dove-admits-it-missed-the-mark-with-whitewashing-ad

Grizzle, A, Wilson. C, ed. "Media and Information Literacy for Teachers." UNESCO, Paris, 2011. www.unesco.org/new/en/communication-and-information/resources/publications-and-communication-materials/publications/full-list/media-and-information-literacy-curriculum-for-teachers

Media Smarts "Advertising All Around Us—Lesson." http://mediasmarts.ca/lessonplan/advertising-all-around-us-lesson

Bibliography

Klemm, William R. "How Advertisers Get You To Remember Ads." Psychology Today, 2014. www.psychologytoday.com/blog/memory-medic/201402/how-advertisers-get-you-remember-ads

Mishra, Neha & Hall, Robert. "Bleached girls: India and its love for light skin." The Conversation, 2017. https://theconversation.com/bleached-girls-india-and-its-love-for-light-skin-80655

Nelson, Kai. "Where's the Representation?: The Impact of White Washing on Black Children." Scholars Archive at Johnson & Wales University, 2016. http://scholarsarchive.jwu.edu/cgi/viewcontent.cgi?article=1037&context=ac_symposium

"New Ad Trend: Selling Through Smelling." National Public Radio, 2007. www.npr.org/templates/story/story.php?storyId=10069425

Poggi, Jeanine & Schultz, E.J. "How Coca-Cola's 'American Idol' Deal Transformed TV Advertising." AdAge, 2014. http://adage.com/article/media/coke-s-american-idol-deal-transformed-tv-advertising/296309

Sweney, M. Protein World Beach Body Ready. The Guardian, 2015. www.theguardian.com/media/2015/jul/01/protein-world-beach-body-ready-ads-asa

Torgovnick May, Kate. "10 brand stories from Tim Leberecht's TEDTalk." TEDBlog, 2012. https://blog.ted.com/10-brand-stories-from-tim-leberechts-tedtalk

Wilcox, D., Cameron, G. & Reber, B. Public Relations Strategies and Tactics (11th Edition). Pearson Education Inc., Glenview IL, 2014.

Chapter 4

"15 top campaigns." Ad Age. http://adage.com/lp/top15

"A History of Bad Taste." Buckley's. www.buckleys.ca/about/history

"About Greenwashing." Greenwashing Index, 2018. www.greenwashingindex.com/about-greenwashing

Advertising Educational Foundation. http://aef.com/classroom-resources/educational-materials

Advertising Self-Regulatory Council. www.asrcreviews.org

Advertising Standards Canada. www.adstandards.com/en

Briggs. Christian. "BlendTec Will It Blend? Viral Video Case Study." SocialLens, 2009. www.socialens.com/wp-content/uploads/2009/04/20090127_case_blendtec11.pdf

Campaign for a Commercial-Free Childhood. http://commercialfreechildhood.org

Cichowski, Heather. "This 18-Year-Old Wrote A 'Brown Girls' Guide to Beauty,' Encouraging Us To 'Love All Shapes and Shades.'" A Plus, 2017. http://aplus.com/a/aranya-johar-a-brown-girls-guide-to-beauty-poem-video?no_monetization=true

Concerned Children's Advertisers. "House Hippo." YouTube, 1999. www.youtube.com/watch?v=TijcoS8qHIE

Cox, R. Environmental Communications and the Public Sphere. SAGE Publications, Inc., Thousand Oaks, California, 2013.

Federal Communications Commission, USA, www.fcc.gov/media#block-menu-block-4

Interactive Advertising Bureau. www.iab.com

Johar, Aranya. A Brown Girls' Guide to Beauty. YouTube, 2017. www.youtube.com/watch?v=ZX5soNoPiIl

Mosendz, Polly. "Coca-Cola Life is Green, Natural, and Not Good for You." The Atlantic, 2014. www.theatlantic.com/business/archive/2014/06/coca-cola-life-isnt-actually-good-for-you/372962

O'Brien, G. Marketing to Children: Accepting Responsibility, Business Ethics, May 31, 2011, http://business-ethics.com/2011/05/31/1441-marketing-to-children-accepting-responsibility

Office of Consumer Protection, Quebec. www.opc.gouv.qc.ca/en/consumer/topic/illegal-practice/advertising-children

Truth in Advertising, www.truthinadvertising.org

Whitehead, Chris. "Coca-Cola Life Arrives in Canada." Coca-Cola, 2016. www.coca-cola.ca/stories/cokelife

Wilcox, B., et al. "Report of the APA Task Force on Advertising and Children." American Psychological Association, 2004. www.apa.org/pi/families/resources/advertising-children.pdf

Learning More

Books

Hicks, Aubrey. *Advertising: Does Advertising Tell the Truth?* (Debating the Issues). Cavendish Square, 2014.

Graydon, Sheri. *Made You Look: How Advertising Works and Why You Should Know.* Annick Press, 2003.

Raum, Elizabeth. *Let's Think About the Power of Advertising.* (Heinemann InfoSearch). Heinemann Raintree, 2014.

Websites

Advertising Educational Foundation
A series of behind-the-scenes videos on market research.
http://aef.com/classroom-resources/educational-materials/

Center for Media Literacy
Tips and questions on how to analyze an advertisement.
www.medialit.org/reading-room/how-analyze-advertisement

Federal Trade Commission
The FTC has created the Admongo games and lesson plans to teach about advertising.
Admongo lesson plans
www.consumer.ftc.gov/Admongo/lesson-plans.html
Admongo game
www.consumer.ftc.gov/Admongo/index.html

Media Smarts
Check out these educational games that help you practice your media literacy skills.
http://mediasmarts.ca/digital-media-literacy/educational-games

Key to Media's Hidden Codes
Excellent video from TED ED on decoding advertising messages.
https://ed.ted.com/lessons/the-key-to-media-s-hidden-codes

TerraChoice
Read about the seven categories of greenwashing. Then, take the "Name that Sin" quiz.
www.sinsofgreenwashing.com

Glossary

agency A group, such as a business, that provides a service or acts on another's behalf

artificial Materials that are human-made, or not natural

brand A company name or image that makes it different from the competition

broadcasted Transmitted or sent over television or radio

channel Types of communication such as TV or newspapers

classical conditioning A learning process by which people or animals learn to associate one thing with another

consolidated Combined many things together to create one whole

consumer A buyer of goods and services for personal use

cookies Data collected by an Internet browser about a person's information or their Internet usage

data Facts and statistics collected together to be analyzed for meaning

decode Change a message into something that can be understood

direct marketing Selling directly to the public, such as through mail order, rather than selling in stores

embellish To exaggerate the worth of something, or make something seem more interesting

encode Change a message into code, or something that is hidden

ethics A standard of behavior with clear rules for right and wrong

fulfill Achieve or satisfy

gender Different from sex; the state of being male or female related to social constructs

guerrilla marketing A cheap and unconventional marketing technique used to achieve maximum exposure

icon A person or thing that acts as a symbol of something

implied Suggested, without explicitly stating

lifestyle The way a person lives; can describe advertising that associates products with a certain desirable lifestyle

marketing Promoting or selling products and services

mass communication Reaching large groups of people through the media

mass marketing Advertising to large groups of people through the media

media All of the ways of mass communication, such as broadcasting and the Internet

millennial The generation of people who will reach adulthood in the early 21st Century

overt Plainly or obviously apparent; not hidden in any way

persuasive Able to convince someone to believe a certain argument

printing press A machine that prints text or pictures on paper by pressing ink down using type or plates

product Something produced or made for sale

public relations The professional upkeep of a company's public image

public service ad A message to the public that is meant to raise awareness or inspire a change in attitudes and behaviors

race A group of people who share the same physical characteristics, history, culture, and ancestors

racism Prejudice or discrimination based on someone's race, often with the belief that one's own race is superior to another

service Doing work for someone

skeptical Not easily convinced

slogan A familiar phrase or sentence that goes with a company name

stereotype A standard idea of a person or thing that can be too simple to describe them properly

target market A smaller segment of the general population than target audience

transparency Making something clear and open to view

United Nations An international organization made up of 193 member states, meant to establish and maintain world peace and cooperation

vague Not clear or precise

Index

About the Author

Susan Brophy Down is a former marketing manager and newspaper writer who has published four other books for youth. Even though she knows how advertising works on the emotions, some commercials can still make her cry.